BROWNIE

JOKES

This book
belongs to

.....Megan J......

BEST BROWNIE JOKES

collected by Brownies
illustrated by Shelagh McGee

RED FOX

A Red Fox Book

Published by Random House Children's Books
20 Vauxhall Bridge Road, London SW1V 2SA

A division of Random House UK Ltd
London Melbourne Sydney Auckland
Johannesburg and agencies throughout the world

Text © Beaver Books 1984
Illustrations © Shelagh McGee 1984

1 3 5 7 9 10 8 6 4 2

First published as More Brownie Jokes by Beaver Books in 1984

Red Fox edition 1999

Printed and bound in Norway by AIT Trondheim AS

RANDOM HOUSE UK Limited Reg. No. 954009

ISBN 0 09 926704 7

FOREWORD

Previously published as *More Brownie Jokes*, all the jokes in this book were sent in by Brownie Guides to their Regional Headquarters. Occasionally a very popular joke appeared more than once, in which case it was attributed to the Pack who sent it in first.

Once again, many thanks to all those who contributed and happy reading!

First Brownie: Shall I tell you the one about the butter?
Second Brownie: Butter not, I might spread it.

80th Bradford Pack

Why did the Brownie put her bed in the fireplace?
Because she wanted to sleep like a log.

1st Muckamore Pack

First Brownie: What is the 25th letter of the alphabet?
Second Brownie: Y.
First Brownie: Because I asked you.

80th Bradford Brownie Pack

First Brownie: Did you hear about the plastic surgeon who stood by the fire?
Second Brownie: No.
First Brownie: He melted.

West Fife Brownies

Why did the Brownie place a loaf of bread in her comic?
Because she liked crumby jokes.

8th West Fife Pack

What has eyes but cannot see?
A potato.

West Fife Brownies

How many cowboys are there in a tin of tomatoes?
None – they're all redskins.

6th and 6thA West Fife Pack

Why did the orange stop in the middle of the road?
Because it ran out of juice.

15th Accrington Pack

There were two eggs in a pan. One egg said to the other: 'It's hot in here.' The other said, 'Wait till you get outside. They'll bash your head in!'

Breconshire County Pack

First Brownie: Have you heard the story of the three eggs?
Second Brownie: No.
First Brownie: Two bad.

3rd Pickering Brownie Pack

Why did the egg go into the jungle?
Because it was an eggsplorer.

1st Annan Brownie Pack

Why did the tomato run?
To ketchup.

3rd Pickering Pack

What do you give a hurt lemon?
Lemonade, of course.

1st Friockheim Pack

What is small, green and does good turns?
A cub sprout.

1st Muckamore Pack

What sort of shoes are made out of banana skins?
Slippers.

Salford Division

What are egg shells used for?
To keep eggs together.

1st Larne Pack

What runs round the garden at 100 mph?
A runner bean.

1st Spennithorne Pack

Knock knock
Who's there?
Europe.
Europe who?
Europe early.

2nd Pendlebury St Augustine's Pack

Knock knock
Who's there?
Ivor.
Ivor who?
Ivor a good mind not to tell you.

1st Strabane Pack

Knock knock
Who's there?
Egbert.
Egbert who?
Egbert no bacon.

1st Spennithorne Brownie Pack

Knock knock
who's there?
Alick.
Alick who?
Alick my lollipop.

2nd Stokesley Brownie Pack

What is grey, has four legs and a trunk?
A mouse on holiday.

87th Salisbury Pack

Once a rabbit felt hungry so he went to the pub
and asked if they sold things to eat. The barman
replied: 'Toasties: Ham or cheese and tomato.'
The rabbit had a ham toastie and a pint of beer.
When he had eaten this he asked for a cheese and
tomato toastie. When the rabbit finished this he fell
down dead.
That evening the ghost of the rabbit appeared.
The barman asked him what he had died of, and
the rabbit replied: 'Mixin Ma Toasties'.

West Lancashire County

Where do hamsters come from?
Hamsterdam.

4th Eastcote Pack

What animal is found on every legal document?
A seal.

Salford Division

What do apes cook their lunch on?
Gorillas.

6th and 6thA West Fife Pack

What are assets?
Little donkeys.

Clackmannan Packs

What did the kangaroo say when its baby went missing?
Someone's picked my pocket!

74th Dundee Pack

Why did the tortoise beat the hare?
Because there is nothing faster than Shell.

55th 'A' Belfast Pack

What goes to sleep with its shoes on?
A horse.

2nd Dingwall Pack

What did the horse say when he got to the end of his bag?
That's the last straw.

Ayrshire South Brownies

Where do horses go when they are sick?
Horsepital.

55th 'A' Belfast Pack

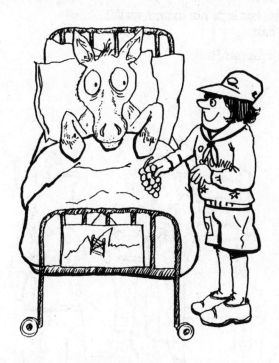

Why did the farmer call his pig Ink?
Because it kept running out of its pen.

1st Claudy Pack

What lion can't roar?
A dandelion.

1st Strabane Pack

What has sixty keys but can't open any doors?
A piano.

87th Salisbury Pack

What has legs but cannot walk?
A chair.

4th Walmer Pack

Why is a piano like an eye?
Because both are closed when their lids are down.

17th Rugby Pack

What did the bubble gum say to the carpet?
I'm stuck on you.

West Fife Brownies

If a blue house is made of blue bricks and a red house is made of red bricks and a yellow house is made of yellow bricks, what is a green house made of?
Glass.

1st Muckamore 'B' Pack

What pie can fly?
A magpie.

1st Annan Pack

Sarah: Do you know you have a hot-dog behind your ear?
Lynette: Oh no! I must have eaten my pencil for lunch.

1st Muckamore 'B' Pack

What did the mayonnaise say to the refrigerator?
Close the door – I'm dressing.

Kent East Pack

What do pixies have for tea?
Fairy cakes.

1st Claudy Pack

What's yellow, soft and goes round and round?
A long-playing omelette.

1st Annan Pack

What is abundance?
A disco for cakes.

10th Dunfermline Pack

What type of thief steals meat?
A hamburglar.

Kent East Brownies

Diner: Waiter, what soup is this?
Waiter: It's bean soup.
Diner: I don't care what it's been, what is it now?

1st Borth Pack

Diner: Waiter, this coffee is terrible – it tastes like earth.
Waiter: Yes sir, it was ground yesterday.

3rd Cyncoed Pack

What did the cannibal say when his friend was late for supper?
Everyone's eaten.

87th Salisbury Pack

How do you make gold soup?
With twenty two carrots.

1st Annan Pack

If bricks make walls, what do walls make?
Ice cream.

8th Fife Pack

What stays hot in the fridge?
Mustard.

3rd Pickering Brownie Pack

Knock knock.
Who's there?
Cook.
Cook who?
That's the first one I've heard this year.

Pixies of 2nd Leyburn Pack

Knock knock
Who's there?
Tarmac.
Tarmac who?
Tarmac kangeroo down sport!

West Fife Brownies

Knock knock
Who's there?
Witches.
Witches who?
Witches the way to go home?

193rd City of Edinburgh Pack

Knock knock
Who's there?
Jaws.
Jaws who?
Jaws one cornetto. . . .

6th and 6thA West Fife Pack

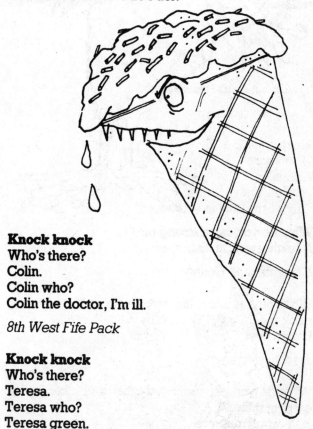

Knock knock
Who's there?
Colin.
Colin who?
Colin the doctor, I'm ill.

8th West Fife Pack

Knock knock
Who's there?
Teresa.
Teresa who?
Teresa green.

80th Bradford North Pack

**What do you call a strong bird?
A featherweight champion.**

Clackmannan County

**What bird is blue, has two legs, and is a hoot at
pack meetings?
Brown Owl.**

1st Claudy Pack

**What do you get when you cross a chicken with a
cement mixer?
A layer of concrete.**

1st Rhyl Pack

Why did the chicken leave home?
Because it was tired of being cooped up

1st Kingsmuir Brownie Pack

What kind of crow never flies?
A scarecrow.

Stockport County Packs

When is a turkey like a ghost?
When it's a goblin.

1st Turiff Pack

What do you get if you cross an owl with a skunk?
A bird that smells but doesn't give a hoot.

Ayrshire South Brownies

What do you call an elephant that flies?
A jumbo jet.

1st Larne Pack

Can elephants jump higher than lamp-posts?
Yes. Lamp-posts can't jump.

1st Larne Pack

What time is it when a load of elephants sit on your fence?
Time to get a new fence.

7th Crewe Pack

Why has an elephant got Big Ears?
Because Noddy won't pay the ransom.

1st Pendlebury St Augustine's Pack

Why is an elephant large, grey and wrinkled?
Because if it was small, white and round it would
be an aspirin.

3rd Cyncoed Pack

What's grey and white and red all over?
An embarrassed elephant.

1st Larne Pack

Why isn't a nose twelve inches long?
Because then it would be a foot.

1st 'A' Dundonald Pack

What did one eye say to the other?
There's something between us that smells.

Pixies of 2nd Leyburn Pack

What has four legs but only one foot?
A bed.

1st Machynlleth Pack

Why do people laugh up their sleeves?
Because that's where their funny bone is.

1st Muckamore 'B' Pack

Why are tall people lazy?
Because they lie longer in bed.

193rd Edinburgh Pack

How high do people usually stand?
Over two feet.

17th Rugby Pack

Why did mummy flea look so sad?
'Cos all her children went to the dogs.

1st Muckamore 'B' Pack

When a fly from one side of the room and a flea from the other meet, what is the time when they pass?
Fly past flea.

1st Rhyl Pack

When insects take a trip, how do they travel?
In a buggy.

1st Turiff Pack

Why wouldn't they let the butterfly into the ball?
Because it was a moth ball.

4th Eastcote Pack

What goes 99 thump, 99 thump, 99 thump?
A centipede with a wooden leg.

Salford Division

Where do tadpoles change into frogs?
In the croakroom.

1st Claudy Pack

What happened to the snake with a cold?
She adder viper nose.

Ayrshire South Brownies

How do you start a flea race?
One, two, flea, go!

3rd Cyncoed Pack

What's worse than a snake with sore ribs?
A centipede with athlete's foot.

1st Turiff Pack

What did the mother glow-worm say to her son's teacher?
Isn't he bright for his age?

1st Turiff Pack

What do frogs drink?
Croaka Cola.

55th B 'A' Belfast Pack

What goes zzub zzub?
A bee flying backwards.

1st Strabane Pack

What did one ghost say to the other?
Spook for yourself.

1st Annan Pack

What kind of fur do you get from a werewolf?
As fur as you can.

Ayrshire South Pack

What does Dracula have for breakfast?
Ready neck.

1st Larne Pack

What do they call Dracula?
A pain in the neck.

1st Annan Pack

What do you call a space magician?
A flying saucerer.

1st Annan Pack

Why is a vampire easy to feed?
Because he eats necks to nothing.

1st Froickheim Pack

What do ghosts call their navy?
Ghost Guards.

1st Larne Pack

Where does Dracula get his jokes from?
His crypt writer.

44th Belfast Pack

Who snoops around graveyards with a magnifying glass?
Sherlock Bones.

Breconshire County Pack

Knock knock
Who's there?
Tick.
Tick who?
Tick 'em up, I'm a tongue-tied cowboy.

Clackmannan County Pack

Knock knock
Who's there?
Justin.
Justin who?
Justin time for the party!

1st Pendlebury St Augustine's Pack

What ring is square?
A boxing ring.

8th West Fife Pack

Does this pen write under water?
Yes, and lots of other words too.

4th Walmer Pack

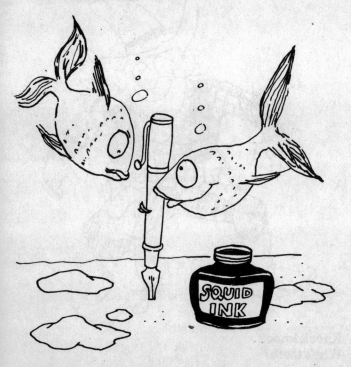

What has an eye but cannot see?
A needle.

1st Annan Pack

What's blue and wears a red scarf?
A freezing snowman.

1st Machynlleth Pack

How many balls of string would it take to reach
from the earth to the moon?
Only one if it was long enough.

1st Machynlleth Pack

What did the envelope say to the stamp?
Stick with me and we'll go places.

1st Muckamore Pack

What did the puddle say to the rain?
Drop in again sometime.

1st Annan Pack

What goes round a field but doesn't move.
A hedge.

74th Dundee Pack

When is water like fat?
When it's dripping.

Salford Division

What runs but cannot walk?
Water.

1st Crossford Pack

What colours would you paint the sun and the wind?
The sun – rose and the wind – blue.

County of Stockport Brownies

What often falls but never gets hurt?
Rain.

7th Ilkeston Pack

What do you call a dentist surgery?
A filling station.

West Fife Brownies

What magazines do gardeners read?
The Weeders Digest.

Breconshire County Pack

What is the only business you can see through?
Window cleaning.

209th Edinburgh Pack

What do you call a Scottish cloakroom attendant?
Angus Coatup.

44th Belfast Pack

What do you call an Indian cloakroom attendant?
Mahatma Coat.

44th Belfast Pack

Why was the farmer cross?
Someone trod on his corn.

Clackmannan County Brownies

What did the fireman's wife find on Christmas day?
A ladder in her stocking.

1st Dunfermline Pack

A sheriff rode into town one day and asked the people, 'Have you seen a cowboy wearing a paper hat and shirt?'
'No,' they replied, 'what's he wanted for?'
'Rustlin'.'

1st 'A' Dundonald Pack

How do fish count?
On fish fingers.

1st Kingsmuir Pack

How are the fish today, angler?
I don't know. I've dropped a line but they haven't
answered yet.

Ayrshire South Brownies

What goes up a river at 80 mph?
A motor pike.

19th Ilkeston Pack

Why did the biscuit cry?
Because its mother had been a wafer so long.

1st Crossford Pack

What is the best thing to put in a tart?
Teeth.

1st Machynlleth Pack

Diner: This lobster has only one claw.
Waiter: He must have lost one in a fight, sir.
Diner: In that case, I'll have the winner.

3rd Cyncoed Pack

How do you start a pudding race?
Sa-go.

Clackmannan Packs

Judge: Order, order in court!
Criminal: I'll have fish and chips, two rounds of toast, and a pot of tea please.

Breconshire County Pack

Daughter: But Mum, I don't like cheese with holes.
Mother: Well eat the cheese, and leave the holes on the side of your plate.

1st Strabane Pack

Where do fish learn to play?
At plaice school.

1st Dundonald Pack

What is a beetroot?
A potato with very high blood pressure.

1st Pendlebury St Augustine's Pack

What swings from cake to cake?
Tarzipan.

8th West Fife Pack

Why did the tomato blush?
Because he saw the salad dressing.

3rd Bearsden Pack

Why are eggs like bricks?
Because they have to be laid.

80th Bradford North Pack

Patient: Doctor, doctor can you help me out?
Doctor: Certainly, which way did you come in?

Clackmannan Packs

A boy with an elephant on his head went to see a doctor. The doctor said, 'Wow, you really need help.'
'You said it,' the elephant cried, 'get this kid off my foot!'

1st Borth Pack

Patient: Will my chickenpox be better next week?
Doctor: I don't like making rash promises.

1st Broth Pack

Patient: Doctor, doctor, I feel like a bell.
Doctor: Give me a ring when you feel better.

2nd Pendlebury Pack

Patient: Doctor, doctor, I keep seeing pink and blue elephants.

Doctor: Have you seen a psychiatrist?

Patient: No, only pink and blue elephants.

Breconshire County

Patient: Doctor, doctor, I feel like a pair of curtains.

Doctor: Pull yourself together.

2nd Pendlebury St Augustine's Pack

Patient: Doctor, doctor, my nose keeps running. I don't know what to do.

Doctor: Well stick your foot out in front of you and trip it up.

26th Bradford North Pack

Patient: Doctor, doctor, I feel like a window.
Doctor: Just tell me where your pane is.

8th West Fife Pack

Patient: Doctor, doctor, I feel like a snooker ball.
Doctor: Be patient and go to the end of the cue.

1st 'A' Dundonald Pack

Patient: Doctor, doctor, I feel like a pack of cards.
Doctor: Well, don't shuffle about, I'll deal with you later.

1st Dundonald Pack

Patient: Doctor, doctor, everyone ignores me.
Doctor: Next please!

Breconshire County

Teacher: Can you tell me something about the great chemists of the seventeenth century?
Pupil: Yes sir – they're all dead.

1st Kingsmuir Pack

Teacher: Julie, why are you crawling?
Julie: But miss, you said I must never walk in late.

1st Crossford Pack

Telephone conversation:
Teacher: You say Tommy has a cold and can't come to school – who am I speaking to?
Tommy: This is my father.

1st Broth Brownie Pack

Teacher: What family does the rhinoceros belong to?
Pupil: I don't know miss, nobody in our street has one.

1st Rhyl Pack

What do elves do after school?
Gnome work.

1st Machynlleth Pack

What is the difference between a train minder and a teacher?
One minds the train and the other trains the mind.

2nd Llanishen Pack

Did you hear about the cross-eyed teacher?
She couldn't control her pupils.

1st Annan Pack

First Boy: Do you think the teacher likes you?
Second Boy: Yes, she puts kisses all over my book.

1st Crossford Pack

How much is 5Q + 5Q?
10Q.
You're welcome!

1st Pendlebury St Augustine's Pack

What did the man say when he found out he was going bald?
Hair today, gone tomorrow.

8th West Fife Pack

What did the hat say to the scarf?
I'll go on ahead, you hang around.

8th Melton Mowbray Pack

What did the wig say to the head?
I've got you covered.

1st Annan Pack

What did they give to the man who invented door knockers?
The Nobel Prize.

6th and 6th 'A' West Fife Pack

Who was the fastest runner in history?
Adam. He was the first in the human race.

8th West Fife Pack

Where are English kings crowned?
On their heads.

1st Annan Pack

First Brownie: Do you know the difference between a post-box and an elephant with gout?
Second Brownie: No, I don't.
First Brownie: I'm not sending you to post any letters.

1st Great Ayton Pack

When do elephants have eight feet.
When there are two of them.

4th Eastcote Pack

What's the difference between an elephant and a slice of bread?
Have you ever tried dipping an elephant in an egg?

1st Crewe Pack

What do you get if you cross a fish with an elephant?
Swimming trunks.

2nd Llanishen Pack

Why does an elephant paint his feet yellow?
So he can hide upside down in custard.

1st Hessle Pack

What's black and dangerous and lives up a tree?
A crow with a sub-machine gun.

Clackmannan County Packs

What do you get when you cross a lawn-mower
with a budgie?
Shredded tweet.

8th Musselburgh Pack

Why is the sky so high?
So the birds don't bump their heads.

Ayrshire South Brownies

What bird has no beak?
A ladybird.

Stockport County Brownies

What goes black and white, black and white, black and white?
A penguin rolling downhill.

4th Eastcote Pack

When is a bus not a bus?
When it turns into a street.

1st Airlie and Ruthuen Pack

Lady: Call me a taxi my good man.
Man: Certainly madam, 'You are a taxi.'

1st Spennithorne Brownie Pack

What was the tortoise doing on the M1?
About 2 mph.

Cairw District Pack

Why do you rest your bike against the wall?
Because it is two-tyred.

1st Darley Abbey Pack

First man: My car had wooden wheels, wooden seats, and a wooden engine.
Second man: No wonder it wooden go!

1st Nonington Brownie Pack

**What is the best thing to take if you are run over?
The number of the car that hit you!**

17th Rugby Pack

**What is black and white and highly dangerous?
A vicar on a skateboard.**

19th Ilkeston Pack

**How do you get to Tenby?
1b, 2b, 3b, 4b, 5b, 6b, 7b, 8b, 9b, 10b!**

2nd Llanishen Pack

Knock knock
Who's there?
Bernadette.
Bernadette who?
Bernadette all my dinner and I'm starving!

7th Bathgate Pack

Will you remember me tomorrow? (yes)
Will you remember me in a week? (yes)
Will you remember me in a month? (yes)
Will you remember me in a year? (yes)
Knock knock
Who's there?
Forgotten me already?

15th Accrington Pack

Knock knock
Who's there?
Doctor.
Doctor who?
How did you guess?

1st Claudy Pack

Knock knock
Who's there?
Isabelle.
Isabelle who?
Isabelle necessary on a bicycle?

15th Accrington Pack

Knock knock
Who's there?
Senior.
Senior who?
Senior so nosy, I'm not going to tell you.

8th West Fife Pack

Knock knock
Who's there?
Cow go.
Cow go who?
Cow go moo, not who!

44th Belfast Pack

What is the best belt to wear on a boat?
A life-belt.

1st Combs Pack

Lady swimming: Help, help! There's a shark!
Boy in boat: Don't worry miss, it's a maneater.

1st Spennithorne Brownie Pack

What is the nicest ship of all?
Friendship.

7th Crewe Pack

Why does the ocean roar?
You would too if you had lobsters in your bed.

3rd Bearsden Pack

What horse doesn't wear a saddle?
A seahorse.

Ayrshire South Brownies

When is a black dog not a black dog?
When it's a greyhound.

Ayrshire South Brownies

What's worse than raining cats and dogs?
Hailing taxis.

1st Annan Pack

What do you call a cat who wants to join the ambulance service?
A first aid kit.

1st Rhyl Pack

If your cat ate a lemon, what would she become?
A sourpuss.

1st Turiff Pack

Why did the boy call his pet dog Smithy?
Because every time somebody called, the dog made a bolt for the door.

11th Arbroath Pack

Why did the man buy a black and white dog?
He thought the licence would be cheaper.

1st Claudy Pack

If a dog loses his tail where does he get another?
From the re-tail shop.

Salford Division

Why does a dog bark?
Because if it meowed it would be a cat.

1st Larne Pack

How many jelly babies can you fit into an empty jar?
None – or the jar wouldn't be empty, would it?

1st Pendlebury St Augustine's Pack

Why did the jelly wobble?
Because it saw the milk shake.

7th Crewe Pack

What's the best slimming exercise?
Shaking your head when someone offers you food.

209th Edinburgh Pack

What sugar sings?
Icing sugar.

1st Tlaiby Pack

Why is the letter K like flour?
You can't make cake without it.

1st Annan Pack

What do jelly babies wear on their feet?
Gum boots.

1st Annan Pack

What did the bull say to the cow?
When I fall in love, it will be for heifer.

Clackmannan County Pack

What do you get if you catch a sheep in the rain?
A wet blanket.

4th Eastcote Pack

Why has a milking chair only three legs.
Because the cow has the udder.

2nd Chinley Pack

How is the 'g' in August like a shepherd?
Because it is surrounded by u's (ewes).

1st Larne Pack

What do you call a bull asleep on the ground?
A bulldozer.

Clackmannan Pack

What do you call a cow eating grass?
A lawn-mooer.

Clackmannan County

Why did the cowslip?
Because she saw the bullrush.

1st Kirby in Cleveland Pack

Why is the letter V like an angry bull?
Because it comes after U.

Ayrshire South Brownies

What did the goat say when he ate a reel of film?
The book was better.

1st Turiff Pack

Why did the farmer feed his cow money?
Because he wanted rich milk.

8th West Fife Pack

How do you milk a hedgehog?
Very carefully.

3rd Anerley Pack

Why is grass dangerous?
Because it's full of blades.

87th Salisbury Pack

What do elephants play in the back of mini cars?
Squash.

5th Barking Pack

What breaks through a wall and mopes?
The incredible sulk!

7th Plumstead Pack

I say, I say, I say, what did one candle say to the other candle?
I don't know, what did one candle say to the other candle?
Are you going out tonight?

2nd Pendlebury St Augustine's Pack

Who is the boss of the hankies?
The Hankie Chief.

West Ham Brownies

Why was Cinderella dropped from the hockey team?
She kept running away from the ball.

19th Ilkeston Pack

What did Batman give Robin for his supper?
A raw worm.

1st Machynlleth Pack

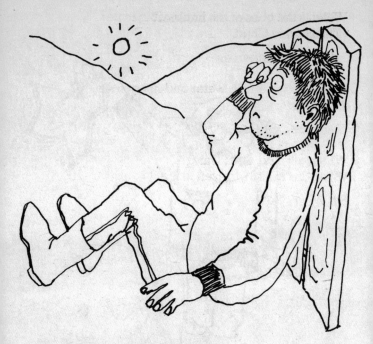

Once there was a man who sat up all night wondering where on earth the sun had gone to. Next morning it dawned on him.

55th B 'A' Belfast Pack

What always walks with its head on the floor?
A nail in your shoe.

1st Annan Pack

When does the day seem short?
When there's a morning mist.

1st Darley Abbey Pack

Which kind of bow is it impossible to tie?
A rainbow.

1st Claudy Pack

What can fall on the water and not get wet?
A shadow.

Clackmannan County Pack

When will a net hold water?
When the water is frozen to ice.

8th West Fife Pack

Why did the policeman cry?
Because he couldn't take his Panda to bed.

3rd Pickering Brownie Pack

What would come up if you dug a hole in the road?
A policeman.

7th Bathgate Pack

What do you get when you cross a bald-headed detective with a camera?
A Kojak instamatic.

Breconshire County Pack

Who chews gum and chases spies?
Bubble-oh-Seven.

West Fife Brownies

Who was the first underwater spy?
James Pond.

Breconshire County Pack

Why did the robber take a bath?
So he could make a clean getaway.

19th Ilkeston Pack

What did the German policeman say to his chest?
You are under a vest!

St James Brownie Pack

What goes up but never comes down?
Your age.

3rd Pickering Brownie Pack

Why did the man climb up the chandelier?
He was a light sleeper.

1st Annan Pack

How do you make a band stand?
Take away their seats.

1st Larne Pack

Why did the Scotsman break a window?
Because he wanted to see glass go.

1st Dundonald Pack

Why are you always tired on April Fools Day?
Because you have just had a March of 31 days.

1st Combs Pack

What question can never be answered by yes?
Are you asleep?

17th Rugby Pack

What happened to the man who couldn't tell the difference between putty and porridge?
His windows fell out.

1st Larne Pack

What goes right up to the door, but never comes inside?
A doorstep.

1st Claudy Pack

Why did the tap run away?
Because it saw the kitchen sink

2nd Pendlebury St Augustine's Pack

When is a door not a door?
When it's a jar.

4th Walmer Pack

Sharon: Did you know that someone invented something that lets you look through walls?
Cathy: No.
Sharon: It's called a window.

1st Muckamore 'B' Pack

How do you keep a house warm?
Paint it with two coats.

West Fife Brownies

What is bought by the yard and worn by the feet?
A carpet.

4th Kirriemuir Pack

Knock knock
Who's there?
You're a lady.
You're a lady who?
Hey, I didn't know you could yodel.

1st Great Ayton Pack

Knock knock
Who's there?
Major.
Major who?
Major answer.

Kent East Brownies

Knock knock
Who's there?
Wilma.
Wilma who?
Wilma tea be ready soon?

West Fife Brownies

Knock knock
Who's there?
Isaac.
Isaac who?
Isaac coming in!

1st Darley Abbey Pack

Knock knock
who's there?
Sam.
Sam who?
Sam one just knocked at the door.
3rd Tranent Pack

Why are carrots good for your eyes?
Well, have you ever seen a rabbit with glasses?

1st Annan Pack

Why do giraffes have such small appetites?
Because a little goes a long way.

1st Maybole Pack

If a husky dog can stand the lowest temperatures,
which dog can stand the highest?
A hot dog.

193rd Edinburgh Pack

How do you get a skunk to stop smelling?
Hold his nose.

West Fife Brownies

What is white, furry and smells of peppermint?
A Polo bear.

1st Maybole Pack

Father bear: Who's been eating my porridge?
Baby bear: And who's been eating my porridge?
Mother bear: Belt-up, I haven't made it yet!

1st Kingsmuir Pack

What do you get if you cross a rabbit with a flea?
Bugs Bunny.

Kent East Brownies

Why is a book like a tree?
Because they both have leaves.

1st Larne Pack

What is the best way to wrap a parcel in an underground room?
Use cellartape.

Breconshire County Pack

In which tree would you hang up your underwear?
In a pantry – or a vestry.

1st Maybole Pack

What did the big telephone say to the little telephone?
You're too young to be engaged.

55th B 'A' Belfast Pack

What can you serve but not eat?
A tennis ball.

Salford Division

Why is tennis a noisy game?
Because every player raises a racket.

2nd Eastbourne Pack